Write a Fiction Book in 4 Weeks

by Drew Becker

Book 1 Interviewing Quick Guide: The Art and the Craft

Book 2 Write a Non-Fiction Book in 4 Weeks

All Rights Reserved. No part of this publication may be reproduced in any form or by any means, including scanning, photocopying, or otherwise without prior written permission of the copyright holder.
Copyright Drew Becker © 2017

ISBN-10:1-944662-16-2

ISBN-13:978-1-944662-16-5

Cover Art by Rockbrand Creative Jennifer Davis

Dedication

This book is dedicated to the great storytellers I have come across in my life. Some have been creative writers; others could just spin a yarn on the spur of the moment and move on. One of my earliest memories is of Matty, a sexagenarian. She took care of my sisters and me when I was still young and our parents were traveling. I was enthralled by how she could tell one anecdote after another and entertain us even more than our favorite kid's shows on TV. I think she infected me with the bug to be a writer.

Many years later my father-in-law Worth Henderson fascinated me with his stories about practicing law in North Carolina beginning in the 1920s, and I have been fortunate to attract people with stories all my life.

Some may have been fish tales while others were embellished versions of personal experiences. I love to hear great story tellers. These face-to-face experiences have been augmented by reading numerous short stories and novels that allowed me to travel without the restraints of space or time. These tales have enriched my life beyond explanation.

Table of Contents

Introduction 5

1. One-Minute Vision 9

2. Four-Minute Foundations 27

3. Eleven-Minute Outlines and Research 59

4. Fifty-Five Minutes of Productive Writing 77

After the Draft 97

Resources 105

Acknowledgments

Thanks to the people who have supported me in my writing and publishing efforts. This includes clients with whom I have worked to publish their books and numerous friends and acquaintances who have purchased other titles in this series.

I appreciate the support from writing clients and those who have published through my company including Regina Oracca, Margo Arrowsmith, W. R. Heustis, Alice Munyua, Tim Chasteen, Michelle Hill, Marie-Anne Lutchmaya, Matt Yablunosky, Inga Martinez, Jennifer Davis, Gary Tomlinson and Miles Kierson, Arielle Stratton, Diana Henderson, Adonal Foyle and Sharon Galluzzo. There are also a handful out there who are still on the journey with me to complete your books.

Other influential people include Pat Howlett, who suggested this might be a passion for me over five years ago, and Martin Brossman, who helped me understand social media and connected me so I could make a portion of my income from blogging. I extend my gratitude to Frank Timberlake for using my blogging services for his company. Appreciation also goes out to Brian and Leslie Brown formerly of Aiken, South Carolina, and numerous North Carolina writers with whom I have collaborated through the years.

Finally, kudos to my wife who is a consummate editor and takes me to task for my misplaced commas and repetitive use of words. She also has endured my absence while I work on my writing projects. Thank goodness she is a writer too.

A Little About Me

I have been a writer as long as I can remember. Before college, I worked in the shipping department of a clothing distributor and was scribbling on the *Inspected by* scraps. While driving a taxicab after graduation, I would take a few minutes between fares to write in my notebook.

In the corporate world, I worked as a technical writer, marketing writer, software support specialist and salesman, and I always found a way to record something during the day, even if only on my lunch break. During that part of my life, I would work on my fiction book at night to release myself from the constraints of more mundane writing. Writing is in my blood; I have ideas floating around my head almost every day and think some of them might be valuable to others.

Since you've found this book, I imagine you have those thoughts flitting around as well, and I hope that you will begin to capture them if you haven't already. You might hear an interesting name for a character or a phrase one of your characters would say. You may get an idea that could move your plot in a new and exciting direction. You might only record a few word, but jot down enough to examine the idea later and decide whether it's worthy of expanding into something more.

My vision for the world is that we live in a less stressful, conflicted environment. I believe that when someone is busy creating he or she has little time to criticize others or increase that conflict. Writers who are not happy with the world around them bring their own to life. This can be one of the great benefits of building a fictional reality. Our day-to-day world might be a better place if more people found their unique creative talents and practiced them.

I left the corporate world just after the events of 9/11 shifted the business climate. The company where I worked was acquired by another one that used this infamous event as a rationale to cut most of us working at their satellite location. I was devastated but decided the time had come to strike out on my own. I'd lived in the shadows of a corporate giant or governmental organization for most of my working life. This time I determined that if anyone would fire me, it would be me.

Even after I left the corporate world and began my own business, I had to create to stay balanced.

I have been writing throughout my whole career. In 1976 I published a poetry paperback and actively participated in the entire process, working with typesetters and printers who had the necessary skills. I learned a great deal about the business of book production. I then took my published work out to bookstores and small shops, created marketing materials and developed the necessary skills to sell my book. I had a chance to see how all the pieces fit together and observe both the creative and business components of the writing game. These early experiences and others along the way served me well when it came time to open my own publishing company.

I also have taught classes and mentored clients in writing. This book is based on many of the lessons I have learned from those experiences and participants. As a former English teacher, before emigrating to the world of business, I had a good foundation in grammar and spelling as well as in composition and logic. I continue to take courses and learn about the art of writing, the craft of publishing both electronic (e-books) and traditional books, marketing and sales, and social psychology.

In this series, I will share as much of my knowledge and experience as I can. This book, *Write a Fiction Book in 4 Weeks*, is intended to help fiction writers produce their books in a short time by completing the first draft in four weeks or a little more. I hope you enjoy the process and appreciate your result.

Drew Becker

Introduction

What is *Write A Fiction Book in 4 Weeks*?

This book is designed to help writers, especially those who are embarking on their first fiction book, to get into the flow of the writing process. I also wrote this book with the intention of helping those authors who started their books and left them incomplete.

Additionally, I hope to present a few ideas to writers who have already completed one or more short stories, novellas or novels. Sometimes even seasoned authors face writer's block or bumps in the road on the way to completing a manuscript.

Writing a book can be daunting. What if you could start with just one minute a day for the first week to get started? This is a guide about how to start by planning and then how to keep going by completing exercises ranging from that one minute for the first week and building to 55+ minutes the final week.

Since many authors face writer's block at one time or another during the process of completing their books, a return to the basics can help. My hope is that using this guide those writers can review the process and this may clear some of their impediments.

I have broken the exercises into four chapters following this introduction. Each of these chapters takes you through a series of seven exercises for the week. One of the major difficulties in writing a book is the continuous effort required. As a result many people begin but do not finish.

Some of the exercises in chapters three and four may take longer than the allotted time. Do not be discouraged and if you only have the allotted time, return to the exercise the next day. Some steps just take longer. Keep moving even if your schedule slips. Follow all the steps because if you skip one, it may have a greater impact on writing or re-writing the book.

For example, if you have a significant amount of research to do, and you begin writing before you are finished with that process, you may have to re-write or delete a complete section in light of the new information you uncover. I am reminded of a writer I know who had researched something historical on the web but when re-writing could not verify the source and—to be true to his audience—had to delete those paragraphs and re-work the chapter, excluding that information.

This can happen even if you have done the research, but you want to minimize the need for this type of rewrite.

Another interruption to fiction writing occurs when characters or critical scenes are left out. Rewriting then can be a major undertaking. Reintegrating one or more characters can be time consuming and demand that the author rework significant sections of the manuscript. Inserting scenes can be done with less effort, but remember to review the impact on plot and character.

What it is not

This is not a book about writing style, grammar or syntax rules. Many writers have already mastered these skills and those topics are beyond the scope of this book. Other resources with that information are available. Some of my favorites are listed on this page on my website, http://drewbecker.com/writing-resources/.

Conventions used in the book

I suggest you create a number of files as you work through the exercises in this book. The file names are written in all caps such as CHARACTER file. This is to help you immediately understand what file is being referenced.

I also have included a fictionalized author whom we will follow on his journey through the exercises. Watching him complete the four-week schedule is intended to make the instructions a little more concrete.

Chapter 1
One-Minute Vision

The idea is as old as the hills. An early version was shared by Wallace Wattles in his 1910 book, *The Science of Getting Rich*. He wrote:

> *Man is a thinking center, and can originate thought. All the forms that Man fashions with his hands must first exist in his thoughts; he cannot shape a thing until he has thought that thing.[1]*

The concept was paraphrased by Stephen Covey when he wrote:

> *All things are created twice; first mentally; then physically. The key to creativity is to begin with the end in mind, with a vision and a blueprint of the desired result.[2]*

In order to bring something into being, we must bring it into the world of our thoughts, and so it is with a book. Thus, the first step in creating your book or your chapter or section is to conceive of it.

By dedicating one minute a day, you can till the fertile ground for your manuscript, and in this chapter I will make suggestions for how to do this. Before you can succeed, however, you must see your book not as a project but as a reality.

Where and when to do these exercises:

Find a quiet place where you will not be disturbed. Schedule the time and make arrangements not to be interrupted. Turn off your phone; close down all social media on your computer or shut down your computer altogether. If you need to make notes, do so with paper and pen or pencil.

Some of the exercises must be done in your writing space; others can be completed elsewhere.

By following this process, you will ingrain the idea of writing your book and also begin to see the end results. As these visions become clearer and more vivid, you will ready yourself to do the actual writing by using the process described in the next chapters.

Until you see yourself as a writer, your task will be more difficult and others will not view you in that role. Having people think of you as an author is critical to the steps necessary to write, edit, promote and sell your book.

The Exercises

Day 1 Visualize

The first exercise can be done anywhere you can find solitude. Visualize your book. Imagine it complete with the picture on the cover, the binding and all the internal pages. Can you see it in the window of your favorite bookstore? Envision a stack of your books on a table or see the spike on your Amazon dashboard indicating a massive number of sales. Hold the picture in your mind for another moment. Make it real.

WRITTEN EXERCISE

Make notes about any thoughts that come to mind. Write them in your FIRST VISUALIZATION file. Print out your notes and title them FIRST VISUALIZATION.

In addition to this exercise, enlist support from family or friends for your writing project. During the next four weeks, you may find that you need someone else to help you keep your writing commitments. Find a person you can turn to at those times. Enlisting a supporter or network of friends also will create accountability. Some of you may want to hire a coach who will make that answerability a scheduled event. When writing a book in a short period of time you might want to be held accountable two or more times a week.

Day 2 Your Writing Area

Set up your writing area. Unlike most of these first-week exercises, this is a physical task. You will need to construct the right environment.

Set up your favorite chair at a desk or if necessary at the dining room table. You will probably be working at a computer. You might also want to have a pencil or pen and tablet or stickies nearby. I also like to make room for my favorite beverage where it will not spill on any electronics or paper. Like many authors, having spilled coffee, tea, water or something else on a keyboard or on notes, I can attest to the importance of this.

NOTE: If you are going to write in a coffee house or outside your home or office, figure out what your set-up will look like. Will you have your phone and/or paper and pencil next to you? Where will you place your laptop or tablet? What else will be on the table?

You will want to get a physical file folder to hold all your notes for your book as you progress through the process. Place your notes from these exercises in your folder. Find a convenient location to put this since you will be adding to it most days through the four weeks. If you will be working outside your home, find a spot inside your computer case or in another carrying bag you will have with you.

WRITTEN EXERCISE

Make a few notes about what you have decided and label this page WRITING ENVIRONMENT. Print out this file and the one from yesterday and put them in your physical folder.

Day 3 Avatar

Today's exercise can be done anywhere you can find solitude. Sit still in your writing area or another serene place and create your avatar.

An *avatar* is a representative of the person who will read your book; in fact, this is the perfect reader. Briefly consider who that person is.

Think of an avatar in the same way you would a character in your fiction book. You need to know that character inside out to discern what he or she will do in the story. You have to understand your avatar in the same way so you can keep him or her captivated.

Answer these questions about your avatar:

What are the **physical aspects** of your reader?

- What is his or her age?
- Does your audience consist of primarily women or men? Knowing this will determine something about your writing. Men generally like a more direct approach based on a logical progression of ideas or events. Women may prefer a richer style with more description and a focus on the people in the book rather than the action.
- Are your readers single and in a relationship, single but not in a relationship, married or committed to a relationship?

Next consider the **psychological aspects** of your reader.

- What kind of attitudes would he or she have based on upbringing?
- How important are home, siblings, travel, freedom, duty, loyalty and companionship?
- What other values are important?

What **habits** would your avatar have? What would please and displease him or her?

What political and religious attitudes does your perfect reader have?

How much does your reader **know** about your settings, themes, type of character? If historical fiction, how much does your reader know about the background of that time period? How much will you have to supply?

Do your readers mostly **work** in companies, for themselves, or do they stay at home?

Give your avatar a **name.**

Even though you may have defined your avatar to a tee, be thoughtful and be inclusive. One strongly opinionated sentence can lose a reader. Try not to offend your audience, especially your avatar.

EXAMPLE:

If you are writing a book of science fiction primarily for men, what do you need to consider about your avatar? You will have to answer a number of questions to get a complete picture of your readers and understand them well enough to know what they expect from your book.

Ask:

- How old is he?

- What is his interest in science, in science fiction, in fantasy?
- Does he live in the city, suburbs or in a rural area?
- Is he an only child or does he have siblings? How many? Do they get along?
- What common interests does he share with friends? What organizations or meet-ups does he belong to? Is he a leader or follower in these groups?
- Is he a loner or a joiner?
- Is he in school?
- Does he have a job; if so, where? Does he work for someone else or for himself? If he isn't employed, what activities fill his days?
- What is the most important thing for him?
- Favorite activity? Least favorite activity?
- What does he read?
- What is his religious background and current practice?
- What kind of political leanings does he have?

- How much does he know about science fiction and about science?
- What is his name?

WRITTEN EXERCISE

You will want to write down some ideas after you think about this exercise. Have a pencil or pen and paper handy, but **do not begin writing** until you have finished building the avatar image in your mind.

Entitle this exercise AVATAR and make an AVATAR file; add the notes to your physical folder.

Day 4 Launch

Visualize your book launch. This exercise can be done in a quiet place. If you have a physical book, will you have an in-person event? Who will you invite? Where will you hold the launch?

If you are releasing an e-book, will you have a web event? Will you plan a virtual book tour? Will you announce it through social media—Facebook™, LinkedIn™, Instagram™?

Will you have a video or do a hangout or Skype™ event? Whom will you invite? What will be the best time of day to attract your audience?

Remember, the more details you include, the better.

WRITTEN EXERCISE

Make notes from your exercise and add them to your physical folder. Title your notes BOOK LAUNCH.

Day 5 Interview

Visualize being interviewed on the radio, a podcast or on TV.

This exercise can be done anywhere that's quiet. Will you be on a radio broadcast? On whose podcast will you be the guest? What TV station will be the first to want to interview this famous or soon-to-be famous author?

WRITTEN EXERCISE

Once again make notes and add to your folder. Title this INTERVIEW.

Day 6 Signing

Visualize signing copies or if you are writing an e-book, emailing signed covers to your readers.

This exercise can be done anywhere you can find solitude. Envision yourself at your live event, sitting at a table with a hefty stack of books at your side and another box nearby. A line has formed in front of you and you are in conversation with fans. You pause and then look down to autograph a few copies with a special remark to each reader.

WRITTEN EXERCISE

Make notes about what you have imagined. Include as much detail as you can. Save these as your BOOK LAUNCH file.

Spending a week with these exercises will help you build a solid foundation and the motivation necessary to keep your writing going.

Day 7 Rest and Review

Take a day away from exercises and see if any other ideas emerge. If so, you may want to record them in one of the files you have created.

Drew Becker

Meet Our New Author, Fiction Writer Dave

Let's examine how this process might work with a fiction writer. We'll follow Dave through all the one-minute processes.

Dave wants to write a science fiction book. He has set aside time and marked it on his calendar and would like to complete his first draft as soon as possible. He is a college student, so he must keep up with his studies while he writes the book and, of course, he will maintain his social life.

Dave sets a schedule for writing in the morning before he studies or goes to class. He is dedicated to the task and will go to the library or coffee house if his roommates get too rowdy.

Let's see how he completes the one-minute exercises.

Day 1 Visualize

Dave sees his book as a sci-fi thriller about an alien invasion that the main character experiences but others don't perceive. He decides to make it a Kindle™ book so he won't have to pay for printing. He can tell all his friends on Facebook and Twitter, and he may use videos to livestream updates as he works on his book. He has enough savvy to know he needs to market before he releases the book. He will have to plan his campaign when he gets close to finishing his first draft.

He already can see the cover with the main character fighting off an alien in a space lock. He visualizes it on the Kindle Amazon site and the Barnes & Noble online store.

Day 2 Your Writing Area

Dave gets up and puts on a pot of coffee. He stretches and then goes to his desk. After clearing the surface, he opens his laptop and brings up his book writing software. He returns to the kitchen and pours a cup then comes back to his desk. He takes out his tablet, which he will use to keep notes that may occur to him but that are not necessarily related to his chapter. He has adjusted his chair to be comfortable but not too relaxed. He places his coffee on a small table to the left.

He hears his roommate Chuck get up and noisily move around the room. He opens Dave's door and asks him where his cup is and begins to recount his adventures from the previous night. Dave asks Chuck to leave him alone for now and comes to a realization. He might have to pack up his laptop and other writing supplies and go to the library or coffee house. He considers what he will take with him and where in the library he could go to be undisturbed. He also will have to turn his phone off if he's going to create the perfect environment. Contemplating this space in the library encourages him and he smiles.

Day 3 Avatar

Dave visits his place in the library after stopping to grab his coffee at the student union. He knows his quiet corner will not have much traffic. He plants himself there with his laptop and his cell. He promises himself not to answer the phone but only to use it to make notes. He begins to think about his avatar: another college student who loves *Star Wars*, *Dr. Who* and Ray Bradbury novels. His ideal reader is 17-25, male, an introvert, watches the Syfy channel, sees most of the superhero movies and likes to consider the world around him as well as fantasize about the future. Seeing this in his mind, he quietly dictates into his phone and begins the file for his avatar. Dave realizes he will continue to develop this ideal reader as he goes and edits the transcription. He reminds himself to record additional information on his phone and transfer to his computer file when those ideas come to him.

Day 4 Launch

Dave gets excited about his book launch. His good friend Jean can help him design a website and do the graphics he has envisioned. He will announce his book and create buzz before it is written and published on Facebook, Instagram and Twitter.

He also will plan a number of Google Hangouts™ or he might use Skype to have another friend interview him about his progress in writing the book and then arrange a large launch party Hangout. Better start collecting names now. He might contact Tim, an actor friend, to read from the book on a Skype call or a Google Hangout. He also considers what other platforms will work for him.

Day 5 Interview

Dave's roommate, Chuck, does a podcast from their room every Wednesday morning. He would want to have a budding author on his show. Another of Dave's friends has a talk segment about the arts on a local radio station. He can imagine himself on both programs. He knows he will have to supply at least a few questions that his friends can ask. In addition, as he already thought, he will set up the Google Hangouts. The interview parts of the launch plan are coming into focus and Dave is feeling more confident. These ideas are also getting him excited about writing his book.

Day 6 Signing

Dave decides he wants to plan a live event the day he releases the e-book. His friend Jean is a great organizer and he takes her to coffee to ask for her help.

"I think we should print copies of the book cover on postcards and give them out. You could sign them. We would need to have some food there and drinks, maybe get a keg of beer, or not. We don't want to have just another drinking party. What do you think?" she asks.

"Good ideas. Do you think we should have Tim do a reading from the book too or should I do that?"

"What if both of you took parts and read a great selection?" she suggests.

"Sounds good to me," he replies, "and we need to encourage people to buy the e-book that day. What if we reduce the price on the day it comes out and maybe the next day or two after? I think that would be good," he says concluding their conversation.

Day 7 Rest and Review

Dave takes the next day off and doesn't set aside time to think about the book. However, he has his phone with him so he can jot down a note if something occurs to him.

Next week Dave will begin his five-minute exercises and I hope you will too.

We will investigate these exercises ourselves in the next chapter.

Chapter 2

Four-Minute Foundations

Congratulations on finishing the one-minute exercises. You now have momentum and can move forward in your preparations.

The next set of exercises each takes four (4) minutes. These will help build a foundation for the book.

Day 1 Purpose

What is the purpose of your book? Knowing the purpose is essential to creating the structure. This is more straightforward for a non-fiction book than a fiction book, but it is important to both.

Since your book is fiction, your purpose could be to entertain or educate, but you need to consider more. What are the themes in your book? How do you want your reader to feel or think after reading your book? Do you dare to hope it could elicit a response?

The actions and thoughts of your characters will be the vehicle you use to present these themes. Mapping out their actions can help to promote these themes and be sure these will emerge in your work.

There are a number of basic themes in fiction based around different types of conflict. In each case the character could be male or female, but for simplicity I will use the traditional word *man* to represent the character (except in number 6). The most common are the following:

1. Man vs. Man—One character confronts and challenges another.

2. Man vs. Himself—A character grapples with social, moral or other issues within himself.

3. Man vs. Society—The character fights the society at large.

4. Man vs. Monster(s)—The character confronts monsters or supervillains.

5. Man vs. Machine—The character fights against an automated enemy.

6. Man/Woman and Woman/Man—The characters encounter and work through relationships with each other.

WRITTEN EXERCISE

Consider your purpose and write it out on a sheet of paper with PURPOSE as the title. Include your themes if you know them at this point. Otherwise, as you work through your exercises, determine one or more as you build your plot. Print out the sheet. Add it to your physical folder.

Day 2 Characters

Your fiction book needs characters to carry out the action. Until you know who your book is about, you cannot begin your story. I suggest to clients that they start by brainstorming who the people in the novel or short story will be. You will need at least two major characters, your protagonist and antagonist and in most cases a supporting cast.

We learn about characters similarly to how we come to know people. The reader watches how he or she thinks, does, acts and feels. Readers can identify with a fully described character because they can recognize that they have things in common. Those who read the book may dream about being or becoming like that character. He or she has fears, hopes, dreams and goals like a living person. Depending on the story, the writer will reveal more or less of this.

Drew Becker

PROTAGONIST

The protagonist is traditionally the hero or heroine. This is the main character whom we follow throughout the story, and this character usually goes through some type of change as a result of his or her experiences. Most protagonists are people but might be an animal and in special circumstances may be inanimate. For new writers I recommend that the protagonist be a person. We need to get to know the protagonist but a full description is rarely presented at the beginning. It is better to come to an understanding about this character throughout the work much like we learn about friends, forming a first impression and then modifying that as we get to know them more and more.

Some protagonists are uncomplicated heroes as we can see in myth, early Greek writing and some children's books. However, life today is not so black and white, so most have flaws and slip into the category of anti-heroes who are more likely a combination of positive and negative qualities.

In contemporary literature, the protagonist is often an anti-hero. Instead of exhibiting the highly moral traits of earlier heroes, he or she is more ambiguous in action, speech and thought. This type of protagonist appeals to today's reader because the complexity of the modern world is incongruent with the traditional hero who is strong, brave and reverent. Instead these anti-heroes share the same flaws as the reader.

From Sam Spade to Tony Soprano, these characters do questionable things as well as performing good deeds. They may break rules, ruin others, commit murder and greater crimes, not necessarily with evil intent but because they are not driven by a moral compass. Sometimes they use the end to justify the means, and if we agree with the end we may forgive the anti-hero, no matter how flawed he or she is.

Anti-heroes are the norm in modern fiction. Some examples we are familiar with are Don Draper from *Mad Men*, Scarlett O'Hara, main character in *Gone with the Wind*, Yossarian in *Catch 22*, Arthur Dent from *Hitchhiker's Guide to the Galaxy*, Holden Caulfield in *Catcher in the Rye* and Brick in Tennessee William's *Cat on a Hot Tin Roof.*

Whether hero, superhero or anti-hero, the reader must be able to identify with the protagonist. In an early manuscript, I created a protagonist who showed no redeemable qualities in the early chapters; my beta readers told me they did not like the book. Someday I may return to it and reveal something besides his alienation to my readers so they can identify with him and won't abandon the book in few pages.

ANTAGONIST

An antagonist is a character who challenges the protagonist. With the exception of graphic novels and action adventure genres, this character is rarely all evil in modern fiction. The antagonist must have some traits we can identify with in order to create a fuller texture and a believable role in the story. In other words, he or she cannot be all bad in the same way a protagonist cannot be all good; instead the antagonist must have a combination of both. When we portray more complex characters, the writer creates a more realistic world.

Few of us know someone who is totally evil. Film often will build this kind of character to simplify the story, but this extreme good-verses-evil format is often less appealing to a reader. Complex personalities are what we encounter in our everyday lives, so we expect the same if our fiction is going to ring true. Even arch-villain Moriarty is admired for his cunning by Sherlock Holmes in the Arthur Conan Doyle stories, and this creates more tension and reader interest than if Moriarty was simply hated by Holmes.

The antagonist need not be as extreme as an arch-villain either. He or she could be a former friend who turns against the protagonist or simply a rival. In any case, this character is as important to the story as the protagonist although he or she may play a lesser role.

SUPPLEMENTARY CHARACTERS

Most stories have a supporting cast. These can be classified into two types, major and minor. The major supplementary characters need to be recognizable for the reader. Each must have some distinguishing traits the reader can use to identify them, and so they stand on their own. Minor supplementary characters need less development.

MAJOR SUPPLEMENTARY CHARACTERS

Foil Character

The foil is used in fiction to contrast with another character—most often with the protagonist. We will refer to the other as the main character for the sake of clarity. By creating a foil, the writer can enhance qualities in the main character. To continue with the Sherlock Holmes example, most of us are familiar with Dr. Watson. He is skilled as a doctor and as a transcriber of the adventures; however, he doesn't have the quick mind to solve the mysteries. The reader relies on Watson's lesser intellect and curiosity to ask the questions the audience wants to know. Watson constantly queries Holmes about how he figured out something from a clue that seems obscure.

If you think of your favorite novels, short stories and films, you will realize the foil is employed often. Go back and re-read or re-watch them and see how these characters are used to build the protagonist or other people in the story.

Sidekicks

Sidekicks may or may not be foils. We have already examined Holmes' Watson who was.

In the *Harry Potter* series, Harry has two sidekicks: Ron and Hermione. Ron is definitely a foil, especially at the beginning of the series. He has a close-knit family, is awkward with his peers and is somewhat dependent. These traits contrast with Harry, who is isolated from his adopted family, popular or at least notorious among classmates and fiercely independent. Hemione, on the other hand, is not a foil in the series. She has traits Harry does not and, although different, adds a dimension to the novels rather than enhancing the protagonist's character.

Job/Professional or School Partners

Many protagonists have fellow characters who share their environment. Some are work or professional partners; others are schoolmates. They contribute to building the world of the main character and are less developed, but they need to have enough substance that the reader can visualize them in scenes where they appear.

Sub-antagonists

The antagonist is often accompanied by others who help him create the conflict for the protagonist. These roles round out his environment and work in concert with him to multiply the challenges for the protagonist and friends. In the case of the *Harry Potter* series, Malfoy's friends, Crabbe and Goyle, play these roles.

The Ensemble

Using a group of characters has gained popularity recently. The characters in an ensemble support each other's actions or are brought together by a set of circumstances as is the case in Agatha Christie's *And Then There Were None*, David Mitchell's *Cloud Atlas* and *Sometimes A Great Notion* by Ken Kesey. This is a challenging way to write because you need to delineate the characters clearly so they stand on their own as strongly as a main character. You will not want to introduce them all at the same time either. The point is to make these characters memorable so your reader can keep track of each of them throughout the manuscript. You may have one stand out and be the protagonist, or each may serve as the protagonist in different parts of the work.

ADDITIONAL MINOR CHARACTERS

Most books have other characters who are less important to the story and the plot. They do not have to be as fully defined. In the *Harry Potter* books, for example, Lavender Brown, Seamus Finnigan and Oliver Wood are recognizable but not deeply explored.

WRITTEN EXERCISES:

Brainstorm your major characters. Make a list of each type that applies to your manuscript. Begin compiling profiles of each one.

> **NOTE:** Go back to the Avatar section and look at the questions about an avatar; you will want to detail these traits and more to build your MAJOR CHARACTERS file.

Print and add it in your physical folder.

When you have completed the major characters, make a list of minor characters and write a less detailed profile for each of them. Build a MINOR CHARACTERS file, and print and put it in your folder.

> **NOTE:** These exercises might take longer than the allotted time. You can complete them this week or later in your process. As new characters surface, add them to your lists and define them to a greater or lesser extent depending on their impact on the story.

Day 3 Perspective/Viewpoint

Another important decision writers make is about perspective. Your choice of storyteller determines how you write the book. There are three dimensions to consider over the next two days: Person and Perspective today and Voice tomorrow.

Deciding how you will tell the story will determine voice, person and viewpoint. If you want a more subjective view, you will express it from your main character's vantage point. You might want to write more objectively and act as an outsider looking on as a narrator. Another option is to communicate it from multiple characters' points of view. Once you have decided on this, you can begin figuring out voice and person.

> **NOTE:** One of the best books to delineate among your choices for these three exercises is *Characters & Viewpoint* by Orson Scott Card.

Person

The easiest way to work through perspective is to select the person first. *Person* is the term many of us learned in English class, meaning whether we're using *I*, *you* or *he/she*.

Person reveals who is telling the story. You have three choices:

First person: A book told from the *I* perspective is presented from the narrator or the main character's point of view.

Second person: *You* stories use what is known as the imperative, where the reader is addressed directly as you. The word *you* is often omitted as it would be in a recipe, which describes how to follow a number of steps.

Third person: Writing the book in third person using *he* or *she* or in rare cases *it* allows the reader to watch as the author tells the story.

Others: This will be covered later in this section.

Let's examine these options one at a time:

First Person (written from the *I* perspective) allows your readers to see your world from that character's perspective. If things occur where that person is not present, you must employ a device such as a conversation with other characters to let the reader know what happened. With the first-person narrative, your work will be subjective, seen through that character's eyes. First person makes your writing immediate and the reader will feel as though he or she is right there with the character. What astonishes the character also surprises the reader in most cases unless your character is less perceptive than your audience. On the other hand, the character may not share all he or she is thinking, and readers may not understand the character's action or speech until they "catch up."

Second Person (written from the *you* perspective) is rarely used in modern writing except in experimental fiction or comedic pieces. *Breaking the fourth wall* to speak directly to an audience can be done with certain types of characters or stories. Groucho Marx did this in a number of films, and Mel Brooks employed the technique in *Blazing Saddles* and other movies. More recently, the main character on *House of Cards* uses second person to address the audience. But it takes a masterful hand to craft second person into a story and make it work. You may want to avoid this perspective unless you are already an accomplished writer willing to take on a significant challenge.

Third Person (written from the *he* or *she* perspective) is useful. The narrator gets to see all the action and can reveal it to the reader as he or she sees fit. The audience watches the action from the same vantage point as the narrator. This view is objective for the most part.

Among the hybrid forms of third person is the omniscient viewpoint where the reader receives an objective perspective but also has access to the inner workings of one or more characters' minds. Larry McMurtry's novel *Lonesome Dove* is an example of the omniscient allowing multiple perspectives to be incorporated.

Some authors change viewpoints in their narratives, but this can be challenging both for the writer and for the reader to understand what is being portrayed. Most authors stay with one point of view. We will consider whether you want to use one or more than one viewpoint in your story.

Add this information to your physical folder. Label the page or pages as PERSPECTIVE 1.

Number of Viewpoints

The next consideration when selecting a viewpoint is number. How many people are telling the story? Do you have a narrator talking to your audience, or is it your main character who shares the plot? Is it both? Do you have more than one character relating the story?

This can get complicated. Many writers do not think about this at the outset and just begin writing; then, when they come to the editing stage, they have to untangle all these viewpoints. Editors also deal with this problem, especially with new writers who have not considered single versus multiple viewpoints before beginning to create a piece of fiction.

Most children's books are written from a single viewpoint because that makes the story easy to understand from a child's perspective. Books for adults also make it easier on the reader when the viewpoint is consistent. Most readers like to share one perspective, that of the main character, but you can also reveal your story through two characters or as described above from the omniscient view.

Add this information to your physical folder. Label the page or pages as PERSPECTIVE 2.

Day 4 Voice

Once you know how many and whose viewpoints you are going to present, you are ready for the next decision. You must create the voice for each perspective. Voice refers to the language and world view of the narrator and/or character(s).

Voice is what the storyteller, characters or writer sounds like. This includes personality, worldview, word choices and other decisions that define who is driving the book from beginning to end.

Voice is critical in your fiction book. Whether you are writing from only a narrator's point of view or from those of one or more characters, voice helps the reader identify with the story. If you have multiple voices (narrator and main character, narrator and multiple characters, or multiple characters without a narrator), each voice needs to be distinct on its own so the reader knows who is speaking or thinking without having to be told every time. Even though you will identify speakers throughout your manuscript, each one should have a recognizable voice.

Each voice has a specific vocabulary that stems from the character's or narrator's personality. That personality is a combination of background, upbringing, temperament, spirit, disposition and other historical, social and personal factors. Voice also applies to how the character/narrator speaks—whether he or she uses contractions, how much local color is included, special phrases that indicate the character, regional sayings and more. Other considerations include speech cadence and complexity of sentences.

Many authors build a character study to flesh out each character before beginning the draft, which is what I recommend. This study can help to identify what the voice should be.

Add this information to your physical folder. Label the page or pages as PERSPECTIVE 3.

Day 5 Structure/Plot

Many writers like to work in an organic way; so the idea of structure is abhorrent or at least foreign to them. I understand this too well and have shied away from any structured approach to my writing until recently. My *just flow with it* process, however, has resulted in a number of half-written fiction books.

Structure has to be viewed as a guideline rather than as a strict, binding form that holds the book and the author in a stranglehold. If the original map does not get the author to the destination where he or she is headed, it is necessary to *recalculate* as my GPS says.

The structure of fiction follows that of the three-act play. You basically begin with the inciting incident followed by a series of crises and recoveries leading to a climax and finish with the dénouement (where loose ends are tied up). The structure of fiction is often referred to as plot.

INITIATING INCIDENT

This is the event that kicks off the story. It is the stimulus and the story is the response. The incident may be substantial like an automobile accident, a kidnapping, a murder or relationship break-up, or it may seem to be inconsequential like an unintentional slight, accidental meeting or a disjointed dream. No matter what this event is, it must come early in the work and be one of the best-crafted scenes in the manuscript. All your action will be triggered by this episode and it will propel your protagonist, so it must be strong enough to launch both your plot and character. This incident is the original conflict in the story.

COMPLICATIONS

In life, very little is straightforward. The same is true for fiction. As the protagonist attempts to work through the original conflict, he or she is deterred from a quick solution. Other events block a speedy resolution. Setbacks help to develop strength and constitution in the main character. These complications of plot can occur as other characters are introduced, as the protagonist discovers new information or limitations are revealed. The antagonist usually gets the upper hand during some of these phases, and it appears the main character will fail. Each additional difficulty increases the tension and conflict.

Each new complication creates a stimulus for the next response and invites the audience to keep reading. As soon as one of these twists is untangled, another one is introduced. Each of the answers brings the protagonist closer to his or her destination, and the introduction of the next solution promises to reveal more that needs to be uncovered until the final resolution.

RESOLUTION

Readers expect some type of resolution in a story. This can be complete or partial, but readers need to come away feeling satisfied. In modern writing the solution may not be complete, leaving room for readers to create their own closure or opening the opportunity for the writer to pen a sequel.

Whole books have been dedicated to plot, and the topic cannot be adequately covered here. I think one of the best resources for learning about this aspect of writing is *Story*[4] by Robert McKee.

When you work on your outline in the next chapter, consider how this affects your plot line.

Add general information about your plot. Label the page or pages as PLOT and put them in your physical folder.

Day 6 Reconsider in Light of Purpose

You have made critical decisions this week about your book. Now it is time to re-read your purpose and themes and contemplate how the various aspects of perspective and structure fit into that. Review each of your choices and determine if they are aligned with the purpose of the book. Has the aim of the book changed as you investigated these other elements?

If all is still congruent, you are finished with this portion. However, if your purpose has changed, make modifications or if some of these elements do not move your purpose forward, change the misaligned ones to match your objective.

This alignment will become more crucial as the book continues. For those of you who have hit a wall in writing, check your work and see if your difficulties are related to the alignment of these elements.

Go back to your PURPOSE file and make any additions or changes. Re-print the file and add it to the physical folder.

Day 7 Rest and Review

Spending a week with these exercises has helped you build a solid foundation to begin your writing. Get away from your computer and reward yourself. Again, see if any other ideas emerge. If so, you may want to record them.

Our Fiction Author Dave

Let's see how Dave works through his four-minute exercises. By this point he has imagined his book, *Zeronicities*, figured out what his traveling office will be like, established his writing environment, designed his avatar, and visualized the launch, interview and signing party. The exercises this week build the foundation for writing his book.

Day 1 Purpose

Dave steals away to his secret nook in the library where he won't be disturbed. He considers his purpose and knows he wants to entertain others about his age. He leans back thinking he has completed this assignment when an incident enters his mind. He was eating lunch when he heard a commotion behind him and saw an older student hassling a younger one from a foreign country for not being able to speak English very well. Dave realizes that he might model better behavior in his characters and a theme emerges.

He begins an inner dialog between himself (Dave 1) and his alter ego (Dave 2).

"I'm going to write my book mostly to entertain," says Dave 1.

"How can I do that? I need to make this clearer for myself," his alter ego, Dave 2, says.

Dave 1 says, "Well, to start with I will need a good plot and a lot of action to keep my readers *engaged*. The book should move as fast as one of my video games."

Dave 2: "That's a start, but what about your characters?"

Dave 1: "Good point. I need some characters my readers can identify with from the start. I guess they ought to have some of the same problems my friends and I have."

Dave 2: "That might work. Now you have to consider what writing the book can do for you."

Dave 1: "I want to begin my career as a novelist, and I would like for people to be impressed that I've written a book. It could get popular and kickstart my career before I graduate. Then I wouldn't have to look for a job. That may not be realistic, but I can dream, can't I?"

Dave 2: "You can dream. You might win the lottery too, but don't quit school until you have written a bestseller. My parents would be furious."

Dave 1: "Yeah, I know. I'm glad I had this conversation since it has helped me to see where I am going. Thanks."

Dave 2. "Now I will print out these purposes and carry them in my wallet to remind me every time I spend money."

Day 2 Character

Dave begins by listing his characters.

MAJOR CHARACTERS

Protagonist

Franklin Trent, main character

Friends of Protagonist

Doug Rattler, a close friend who is a wise-ass and was bullied when he was younger

Bill and Amy, a helpful couple

Antagonist

Mr. Morse (ABZL12)

Associates of antagonist

Tamika, his assistant (BCAM04)

Minions of "the others"

MINOR CHARACTERS

Gregory, Franklin's best friend

Barbara, Franklin's girlfriend

Tim, Earth contact 1

Denise, Earth contact 2

Dave realizes this is a preliminary list and that other characters will surface as he completes the plot and begins writing. He is pleased with his progress and believes that with the identification of the characters the plot is beginning to gel in his mind.

FRANKLIN TRENT PROFILE (Preliminary)

Physical

- Male
- 22 years old
- 6 feet tall
- Chestnut brown hair, brown eyes, triangular face, light eyebrows, muscular, athletic
- Medium length hair
- 175 lbs.
- Thin lips, nice smile

Social

- Biology major at State University
- Plays lacrosse
- Likes to read about athletes
- Writes short stories

Family

- Family lives in Boulder, Colorado
- Oldest of four children – Siblings: Nick, 14, Debra, 12, and Christa, 10
- Father: Jerrod, 47, an executive, absent much of time
- Mother: Lillian, retail manager at clothing store; recently returned to workplace
- Grandparents on both sides are deceased.
- Relatives live in Chicago, Cincinnati and Charlotte.

Psychological

- Optimistic and idealistic
- Middle class (not affluent but not poor)
- Raised outside church but family attended Easter and Christmas services
- Close to Nick but not so much to his sisters
- Has not traveled much
- Average student
- Smart but bored by school – has B average
- Inventive

Drew Becker

Interests

- Lacrosse
- Chess
- Socializing/Partying
- Art
- Entrepreneurship
- Dating

Day 3 Perspective and Viewpoint

PERSPECTIVE

The next day Dave starts the first of the perspective exercises. After forcing himself to get up after a long night of studying and having a few beers with his friends, he heads to a coffee house a little distance from campus so he can be undisturbed.

He thinks back to last month when he was reading *Cat's Cradle* by Kurt Vonnegut. His main character tells the whole story in first person. "I might want to write the book from my protagonist's point of view," he says to himself, "but the more I think about it, that might be limiting. I could do it but I would rather get a wider perspective."

He decides he will tell the story from a *third person* point of view. He will reveal the plot as readers watch the characters in action. He has almost settled on this point of view when he realizes he might want to tell part of the story from more than one character's viewpoint. Upon further consideration, he realizes he needs to use the *third person omniscient* view.

This seems like a good choice and gives Dave the flexibility to delve deeply or more shallowly into his characters. As the story is written Dave can make those decisions. This strategy gives him access to inner dialog of one or more characters and the advantage of first-person narrative without the need to limit his storytelling. What is important is that Dave now has some parameters for what he is writing.

NUMBER OF VIEWPOINTS

How many viewpoints does Dave want to use? He has more freedom using third person omniscient. He will want to step back from the story as the narrator and write about the action; so that's one perspective. He will bring his readers into his protagonist's mind at times. Should he take the reader into the antagonist's mind as well? Maybe, he posits.

So he will use at least two, maybe more, viewpoints to tell the story. He realizes that as he is writing he will have to keep track and be sure not to confuse the audience. He has read books where each chapter is from a different character or the narrator's viewpoint. He might have to get clearer on this as he starts writing, but he knows he will begin with at least two.

Day 4 Voice

Back in the library in his favorite place, Dave thinks about voice. He decides to define the voice for only the narrator and the main character and for now to keep things simple.

The narrator will have his voice. He can hear it in his head naturally and will use that voice although he may add something to it to make it more objective. The narrator sees the entire picture. He shares the story from the perspective of someone who appears to be one of the last survivors on Earth. The narrator will not let the reader know until late in the book that another colony of survivors remains less than 100 miles away. This perspective will color the way he describes the world and may allow him to lend a political feel to the manuscript.

The main character will be heroic and will have flaws. He is estranged from his family. This character's voice may switch between empathy and cool detachment depending on whom he is addressing. He will exhibit bravery and will stand up for those who cannot defend themselves.

Since Dave's audience could be wider than his college friends, he understands his writing must be accessible to all those readers; so he has to be clear. He will use short sentences for the most part. His vocabulary might stretch some members of his audience but not too much. Most of his readers are not going to stop and look up a word unless they are reading an e-book with the dictionary built into their device. Even then many of them are not going to take the time to look up uncommon phrases and words.

Day 5 Structure/Plot

Dave has had a busy day taking tests and preparing for upcoming exams; so he doesn't get to his writing exercises until after dinner. His library corner is quiet and he can work there. With many of the decisions made about how the book will be written behind him, he is ready to think about the structure of the novel. He realizes he needs to consider what kind of event will entice his readers from the first page and works on coming up with an idea of what the first action in the book will be.

He contemplates whether to begin with the narrator or the main character. After a minute of thought, he opts for the narrator so the reader will see this action from outside the character. Now he can begin thinking what this initial conflict might be. He could start with the estrangement from the family but decides he wants more action, more adventure.

He will have to open with something scary or challenging for the main character.

The book will take his main character on an adventure in three parts. Section one will occur on Earth when the invasion begins. In the next section, the action will move into outer space, and the third part will return the hero to Earth where his small band will attempt to regain control of their planet.

He wants to be sure to inject some humor into the story right away and may do that with a minor character or with wise cracks from a major character. In either case, the humorous slant needs to appear early in the book.

Just as Dave is putting his laptop away, Jean comes over and starts a conversation. He discovers that she is a writing a book as well. They decide to meet again and discuss their writing projects.

Day 6 Reconsider in Light of Purpose

With all the details in mind from this week, Dave revisits his original notes about purpose. He pulls his paper out of his wallet and looks at it. Considering everything else he has determined this week, his purpose to entertain with a fast-paced story that might include a theme about acceptance of others still works.

He reviews his personal goal of becoming a successful author and that hasn't changed. In fact, that helps him to commit to continuing with these exercises to build the best book he can. He is satisfied he has put together the correct information to define his purpose for himself and his readers. One more idea pops into his mind: He might write a series. That gives him more reason to do his best in building the characters in the first book and making sure it is something that his audience will want to read.

Day 7 Rest and Review

Dave is delighted with his progress for the week. Today is a play day; no work on the book, no homework. He calls Jean and they decide to get together for a few beers and discuss their writing. However, they talk about other things that they have in common; sharing about writing will have to wait.

Chapter 3

Eleven-Minute Outlines and Research

As discussed in the last chapter, a certain amount of structure can help you with your writing. In this series of 11-minute exercises, we will frame the book. A fiction writer needs to have an end in mind. We discussed purpose in the first chapter which is a good guidepost, and the writer can benefit from filling in some of the stops along the road to direct the writing and stay on course. For fiction, whether driven by character or story, a list of essential plot points is important.

In addition, you might be required to research to gather the information needed to complete your manuscript. You may have to learn more about a setting or a historical event that is included in your story. Research also adds to the texture of characters and helps fill in details about a scene.

Day 1 Outline

Even if your outline is no more detailed than chapter titles, it can help you. Let's analyze how this process applies to your story.

Your outline for fiction includes plot points you have considered that can aid you in beginning your manuscript. My fiction is driven by character rather than plot, but I begin with plot points I want to include. When my characters take me down a different path, I can adjust my outline to follow. I rarely change what I am writing to conform to the outline. This practice occasionally gets me in trouble because I write something that does not belong in the manuscript.

Writers whose work is plot-driven need to produce a detailed outline aligned with what they think will happen. Return to your PLOT file and update it.

Be sure to make a hard copy of this work and replace it in your physical folder.

Day 2 Determining Your Research Needs for the Story

What additional information do you need to flesh out your characters, locations and intersecting events? Readers expect the details of your story to be accurate even in a work of fiction.

For historical novels, correct locations, dates and events are essential. Other fiction must be consistent in presenting all these facets. For instance, in a great spy novel the author may reveal something about how the clandestine organization works and describe some of the tech used by the characters. When the reader learns more about a topic in the book, he or she feels an intimacy and gets the impression of being on the inside. In fact, in his James Bond novels, Ian Fleming included lengthy expositions critical to the book's subject. *Diamonds are Forever* incorporates long passages about these gemstones.

Think through your story and make a list of what you need to research. You may not need to write an essay like Fleming did, but you may want to inform your readers about a topic within your manuscript. In science fiction, your readers will expect that you have researched the science where relevant and that it is congruent with current theories and practices. Fantasy readers may be more forgiving. In historical fiction, the timing of the story should coincide accurately with actual events.

Thanks to the internet, research is somewhat easier today, but be cautious about what you read online. One of the advantages of looking at printed materials is that the publisher may have fact-checked what is written. Blogs and other web publications may be accurate; however, there is a chance that facts in these resources have not been checked. Finding a second source is standard practice in the world of newspapers and is a wise idea for fiction writers as well. You might want to search for a third verified source if you have any doubts.

Write descriptions of the important settings and scenes. You may want to gather pictures so you can refer to them as you describe one of these settings in your book. Is it a city of hundreds of thousands or millions or is it a town or village with a population of thousands or hundreds? How close is the nearest metropolitan area? Is your setting a bedroom community? Knowing this information will make the writing go faster because you already will have data to draw from in your descriptions. Create a SETTINGS file.

Print and/or collect your research and place in your physical file folder for the book.

Scheduling

You will probably not be able to complete this in a day. Set a schedule for doing your research. For fiction requiring deep research, you may have to complete this work before writing, which means the other exercises may be delayed.

Day 3 Continue Research with the Marketplace

You started yesterday by setting the scope for your research. Today continue to gather information so you can be ready to write, advertise and sell the book.

To understand your market, go to a physical bookstore and look online at Amazon or Barnes & Noble to view the categories for your type of fiction. How might your book be classified if it were on the site or in a bookstore? At your local bookseller, scan the back cover and you will see what categories the publisher has chosen for the book. On Kindle for Amazon that information is printed below the book listing.

Grandfather Poplar Kindle Edition
by Diana Henderson ▼ (Author), W. R. Heustis (Illustrator), & 1 more
☆☆☆☆☆ ▼   10 customer reviews

   Amazon Best Sellers Rank: #812,489 Paid in Kindle Store (See Top 100 Paid in Kindle Store)
   #15379 in Books > Children's Books > **Science, Nature & How It Works**
   #18791 in Books > Children's Books > Science Fiction & Fantasy > **Fantasy & Magic**
   #50249 in Kindle Store > Kindle eBooks > **Children's eBooks**

Now delve into what books are in your classifications. Most books have three categories. Check them all for similar novels.

Look at the bestsellers both online and in a bookstore and find out how they are catalogued. You can read the beginning of many online books with the *Look Inside* feature. Discover what other authors' writing is like. I don't suggest that you copy their style, but it is a good idea to see what people are buying.

Special Considerations:

Categories are important for any type of book. You will want to set this up correctly from the outset so that readers can find similar books you will write in the future with ease. Remember who this audience is so that you can focus your efforts to *mine* those prospects.

Audience research can be a lengthy process, so you may need to move some of these tasks to later in the week.

Save your work as AUDIENCE RESEARCH, print out what you have discovered and place it in your physical folder.

Days 4 & 5 Determine Your Research and Continue Capturing It

Once you have your list of the required topics, begin doing your research both for the book and for marketing. These activities usually take more than one session; so I dedicate the fourth and fifth days to this finishing this undertaking. You will want to complete the majority of your research before moving on.

Day 6 Filling in and Revising the Outline

With your research done or nearly completed, you are ready to revisit your outline. You may want to revise your chapters or information inside one or more of them. This is the time to do so before you start your writing.

Re-build or refine your plot list. Remember this does not constrict your writing but gives you a map to find your way through the story. What degree of details you include depends on how well you have planned your story. You can move, add and delete plot points as you go, but try to make this as accurate as possible so your writing stays within the scope of the novel or short story. Shifting a plot point can have rippling effects throughout your book. The later that kind of change is made, the more impact it can have on the rest of the manuscript.

In order to write quickly next week, you need to have a good idea of the timing of events. By referring to your plot points, you'll find it easier to string together these occurrences.

Much modern fiction seems to break the rules about a straightforward plotline. If you are writing in an unconventional style, your plot outline may become even more important. With the structure mapped out, you are freer to move forward in a more creative fashion.

This process of nailing down your plot is vital. Many writers regret skipping this preparation when they have to restructure after completing the draft and need to scour their work to find references and determine what they have written previously.

If you move a chapter to an earlier point in the book, you need to review the material in that chapter and all others affected by the change, because you may have written with the assumption that the reader already knows something that now has not yet been presented.

Print your revised PLOT file to use when you begin your writing next week. Place it in the folder.

Day 7 Rest and Review

You have had a busy week if you have completed all these exercises. If you still have work to do, you may have to adjust your schedule or take time out of your rest day. Even if you do cut into your free time, be sure to get some respite and walk away from the project at some point before beginning the final set of exercises.

Our Fiction Author Dave

Let's see what Dave is doing with his writing this week.

Day 1

After a visit to the coffee bar, he ambles to his favorite place in the stacks and gets settled. The expresso is strong and he is buzzing. He admits feeling a sense of dread about writing the outline. He knows that he can begin by using the sections of the book he determined last week so he gets started:

I. On Earth

II. In Space

III. Back on Earth

So now he has to decide what to do with the "On Earth" section. He has 11 scenes he will write in this first part.

1. The Glimpse

2. Inciting incident: His best friend and girlfriend have disappeared.

3. Gathering his posse to look for them

4. Incongruent clues

5. Cold trail turns hot

6. Meeting Mr. Morse

7. Hell on earth

8. Banding together

9. Stealing a vehicle

10. Becoming fugitives

11. Leaving the atmosphere

He can see the plot begin to take shape as he adds elements to his outline. Even though he has not included any detail, he can discern where the story is headed, and it's no longer just rattling around in his head. He wants to start writing, but he realizes that so far he's having success by following the system; so instead he goes through the process for the next two sections. Once he has completed the entire outline, he still has time. He goes back and begins to fill in the first point, "The Glimpse":

A. The Glimpse
   1. Tossing and Turning
   2. Strange lights awaken
   3. Unfamiliar sounds
   4. At the window
   5. Neighbor's abduction

6. See a saucer?
7. Splashing water on his face
8. Return to the window
9. Normal view outside
10. Imaginary material for a short story or reality?

Dave then takes each subsection and begins to break it down:

Tossing and Turning

- Another sleepless night - "Curses to that cup of Kauai Coffee!"
- Eyes open then close; then try to get back to sleep
- Back to sleep
- Awakened by a feeling
- Back to sleep

Strange lights awaken him.

- Light on his eyelids in semi-dream state
- Opens eyes to nothing unusual
- Closes eyes and tries to sleep until a light interrupts again
- Brightness stirs him

Unfamiliar sounds

- Engine decelerating but not a car or truck
- Steam exhaust
- Like cracking open of a door
- Hydraulic release
- Metal scraping against metal

At the window

- Walks over to window
- Trips on sister's flying saucer toy
- Opens shade
- Eyes adjust to light - blinking
- Sees an unknown vehicle or maybe not
- In and out of phase

Dave realizes he is having fun and that the story is unfolding right before his mind's eye. The alarm he has set on his computer startles him. He saves his file as Plot Outline and closes his laptop. He would prefer to stay and work more on this, but he has class in five minutes; so he gathers up his books and backpack and heads out of the library across campus to his Chem 205 class.

Later in the day he will steal another hour and fill in more of the outline. He wants to be ready for the next day's activity.

Day 2

Dave knows this is a research day and although he has filled in many points in the plot outline, he realizes there is more to do. However, using these plot points, he writes topics he will have to research for the book.

He will need to be somewhat versed in the following:

- Space travel
- Flying saucers
- Lasers and laser weapons
- Telekinesis
- Mind reading
- Conventional weapons for non-military personnel
- Geological plates
- Space stasis
- Locations: Boulder, Colorado; Colorado Springs, Colorado; Jackson Hole, Wyoming; Washington, DC; Greensboro, North Carolina and Boston, Massachusetts.

He knows there will be more items to research but this is a good start. He will have to find extra time again to finish the list.

Day 3

Dave invites Jean on his field trip today. They go to the closest off-campus bookstore. There the two of them pull science fiction books and make notes about their categories. Most are listed as Science Fiction and Fantasy. Jean's book is a historical novel; so they record the categories for her book as well.

Afterward, they grab a sandwich and talk.

"You know, Jean, I have been looking for someone to support me through the process of writing this book and I had chosen my roommate, but he isn't a writer and I don't think he's really into it. I need someone who understands the writer's journey and I think that is you. Would you be my support and accountability partner to make sure I keep going?"

"Sure, I can do that. I want to see your book done and whatever you want to share with me is okay."

"Well, I don't want to share the writing until I finish the draft because I have done that before with someone else and ended up getting sucked into editing. Long story short, I never finished the book. But I can share notes and other stuff with you if you'd like. By the way, can I help you with the historical fiction novel?"

"I'm in the early stages," Jean confided to him, "and not really ready to write it yet. It's just an idea. You know what? If you can get your draft written in four weeks, I'll try the same thing after you're done. In the meantime, just encourage me to keep thinking about my book, all right?"

"Sounds like a plan. Let's finish up so we can go to the coffee house, log onto Amazon and find the categories that match."

Dave makes notes on a sheet he titles AUDIENCE RESEARCH.

Days 4 and 5

Dave meets with Jean again and they look over the research from the bookstore. They explore the *Look Inside* feature online for bestselling sci-fi books, but after a few minutes Dave stops.

He says, "I need to quit doing this. I need to keep my thoughts separate from these other books, but in the few we have looked at I can tell my story is like a number of other popular books in the genre. I want to go back to thinking about other ideas to research. You've read my outline. Can we brainstorm for a while?"

Jean agrees and they spend the rest of the time discovering other topics Dave will need to investigate. He is grateful for the help. They make plans to have dinner together later that night. Dave needs to study but before he does he begins the research on one of the topics.

Dave spends time on the next topic on day five. He is determined to make time over the weekend to do more exploration. Maybe Jean will go with him to the library.

Day 6

Dave is still not satisfied with the outline. He spends day six working on it. Nothing he has researched has impacted the outline he has already composed, but some things seem to be missing. Dave spends his time reviewing and doing minor revisions on the outline. He saves the most recent copy and heads home to do his homework and write two papers that are due soon.

Day 7

Dave asks Jean to go hiking and the two of them are happy to get away from studies and writing for the day. After returning home Dave pulls out his hard copy files for the week and looks them over before getting some sleep.

Chapter 4

Fifty-Five Minutes of Productive Writing

This chapter is for those who have completed the first three weeks and have a good handle on vision, foundations and the outline and have begun research. You are now ready to start writing your book. How many of you already have done that? I know that a number of you got the fever sometime during the vision week. That's fine and a common experience, but I hope you have waited until now after completing the other exercises to begin writing your draft. Now is the time to focus on the writing itself. You may find you have to continue your research during this week as well.

My experience with writing is a funny thing. Once I get on a roll, I want to keep going non-stop without sleeping or eating. Obviously that isn't healthy or sustainable. Be sure not to blow all your energy early and burn out halfway through the race. Creating a book is usually a marathon and rarely a sprint.

In each session try to write for 55 minutes straight without interruption. Please control your urge to answer phone calls, look at social media on your computer or cell or open other applications on your computer. Give yourself this period of time and schedule it the same way you would if you had an important meeting with someone.

Even with the best intentions to focus, you can still be interrupted. If you find this happening, divide your writing time into four 15-minute segments. However, you will need over an hour since each time you break and begin again, it takes a few minutes to get back into the groove.

Regardless of the interruptions, external or internal, remember that this is a commitment to yourself, and if you want to get this work done you will have to keep writing. In addition, *please* avoid blaming and chastising yourself for these disruptions. Let it go. Get back on track and write some more. I know people who spend time having internal discussions about how they have let themselves down instead of returning to the task at hand. If you are interrupted, just resume where you left off as soon as possible.

Another potential problem is having other things pop into your mind while you are writing. You may have a lot on your to-do list outside of working on the book. Let these things go for as long as it takes in this week's sessions in order to get this first draft written.

I am often interrupted during my writing time. When I am ready for a marathon session, I go to that mental space I have dedicated to writing. I have learned to overcome the guilt I used to feel arising from thoughts that I *should* be doing something else. With external and internal blocks erased, I focus and write for the time I have blocked to do so.

Depending on the length of your book and how quickly you can write, you may need more than 55 minutes a day to complete your draft. You are in charge of your schedule. Only you know how committed you are to your book.

One way to determine the time you'll require is to decide how long you want the book to be and then estimate the number of words you will need based on page count. Setting a daily goal keeps me on track. If you are writing an 80-page book, your total word count will be around 20,000. Each page has approximately 250 words. If you want to create an 80-page book, you will have to write just over 13 pages a day or 3300 words. If you can complete 10 pages (2500 words) a day for eight days, that will achieve your goal as well.

Another thing to remember is that if you have just begun on this path, you will become more efficient as you write more. I did not feel like my style matured until after I had completed a 250-page manuscript. I may never go back to edit and publish that book, but it helped me to write faster and improve my skills.

Writing a longer book will take more time. If your number of pages is too large to complete the process in 55 minutes per day for a week, plan to spend more hours each day or more weeks to finish your draft.

Two other strategies are to use voice-to-text software or have your recorded files transcribed. A program like Dragon Naturally Speaking® or Apple Diction® allows you to dictate and then copy the dictation into your book file or files. Most of us speak much faster than we type, so this can save time. Be aware that if you use one of these programs, you might have to make a lot of corrections to the text recorded by the speech-recognition software. None of these programs are perfect. If you need to rework the text, avoid doing edits; just make it intelligible. You also can employ a transcription service. Create the writing by recording your voice and send it to a service to have it transcribed. You will get a digital text copy of your words.

Day 1 Writing from Your Outline

Begin filling in your outline. Some software lets you write in different chapters and keep them all together in that program. The one I use allows me to set up my chapters based on my outline, select the one I want and start writing it or continue working on it. I can then edit that later.

Some writers prefer to use word processing software, which will work too. The challenge may be to keep track of all the chapters and move them when necessary.

Rather than beginning with the introduction or preface, it's easier to jump right into the first chapter. That's where the story is. Introductions are often composed last. Grab your printed outline and start the first chapter on your computer. Write for the full 55 minutes if possible. If you are interrupted, you will want to go back and use the strategy presented earlier in this chapter.

At the end of each writing session, I check my word count. Microsoft Word performs the word count and keeps track at the bottom of the page.

I do not check word counts during my session because it breaks my concentration. I keep a file to track the number of words per day after each session. I use Excel and simply enter the dates and the word count. In the third column, I divide the words by 250 to get a page count. This serves to help me know how well I did with my goal for the number of pages.

NOTE: If you decide to take a day or two or a weekend to do a marathon writing session, you may be able to reach your goal more quickly. Remember to get some rest so you are fresh when you write. During a lengthy session, I get up, stretch and walk around every hour or two. Always be sure to save your file before you leave your writing. If you get tired or feel your productivity declining, take a few minutes to relax or focus on something else. If you feel burned out even after a break, let it go for the day.

Write non-stop as best you can. Do not worry too much about spelling as long as you can understand what you are saying. Although you may be tempted to re-read and re-write as you go, this is a bad idea.

I say this because before I finished my first fiction book I kept reworking the writing. I spent so much energy trying to get the wording perfect that I often lost track of the story and my train of thought. After revising, I would come back and feel like I was starting over again. I was successful in completing my draft only when I wrote straight through without worrying about spelling, grammar and punctuation. I know quite a few writers who have had this same experience.

I find the best method during a session for me is to stay with a chapter until I have finished it. If I complete one chapter in a sitting, then I move on to another. You do not have to write your manuscript in order, but be aware that any information you present in a later chapter must be based on material in a previous one. I will discuss moving parts of your book soon.

As you write, please save your work often. Save more frequently than you think you need to, because the one time you don't, you might lose your work. No matter what software I have used, I have lost writing because I did not save often enough. Even though some programs perform automatic saves, the most recent version or the material isn't always retained.

Once you have written for 55 minutes or longer and saved your work, you might want to reward yourself by looking at your numbers. As noted earlier at the end of each writing period, I record my word count.

Days 2-6

Return to your writing refreshed. Take a moment to switch gears and get into your story. Remember your purpose and who your avatar is. You might have to read the end of what you wrote yesterday, but do not take time to go back through the whole chapter. ***Do not*** start editing because that will eat up today's allotted time. As soon as you can, begin writing again.

In most cases I pick up where I left off, but sometimes I feel inspired to write in a different chapter. Follow your instincts about where you focus your energy. As I said, I usually return to where I stopped yesterday.

Once you have the first day of writing completed, each day that follows becomes progressively easier. With all your previous research and story in mind, continue your writing, moving along as quickly as you can. Sometimes you may need to do some minimal revision as you go. You might add a paragraph before one you've already written or move a paragraph somewhere else. This is fine; just keep going.

Write for 55 minutes or longer, saving as you go, and at the end perform your word count again. Record your numbers and evaluate how you are doing.

Each day you will continue working on the chapter you have started or write in a different one. You may need to stop and do research along the way. Try to finish a section or the whole chapter before you change tasks. Hopefully you completed enough research before you began, but sometimes more investigation is needed as you write.

Researching uses a different part of the brain from writing. We automatically make these switches in everyday life without being conscious of it. However, you need to understand that this shift will take you out of your writing mode. This is necessary in many cases and is not in itself detrimental.

When the research is completed and you are ready to return to the writing, realize that moving between different parts of the brain can affect you. Some writers can more easily switch back and forth between these logical and creative activities, and that's acceptable if it works for them. However, if you find this difficult, you might want to pause for a few minutes, take some deep breaths, maybe get something to drink and/or eat and then re-enter your writing mode.

Although I do not recommend editing while you are still writing the book, it is sometimes required. Only make significant changes if they are absolutely necessary to get through the draft.

As mentioned earlier, it's important to be careful when moving material in your book. This advice seems logical and simple, but you can create a mismatch for readers if you do not consider all the ramifications. You may find that you want to change the storyline and decide to move a chapter or section to another location. You may rearrange paragraphs, parts of a chapter or even full chapters. Some writing software enables you to do this with ease. However, when you move words, paragraphs or chapters, be aware of how that affects the story. These alterations may mean you need to make additional changes in other chapters.

The greatest chance for an issue to arise comes from relocating a chapter to a later part of your book. By doing so, you may be removing references that are essential in subsequent chapters. For example, if you described a meeting between your protagonist and a new character in chapter two, then move it to later in the book, your reader will no longer know about the encounter when the person enters a scene in chapter three. Your audience will be clueless about who the new character is and about anything that took place in what once was a previous scene but now appears in a later part of the book. When you rearrange parts of your writing, you have to re-read all chapters that might be affected and make the appropriate changes. If you can wait until it's time to edit your book, do so, but if this change affects your story as you are writing it, you may have to take care of this during the draft stage.

By positioning a passage to a point earlier in the book, you'll also have to re-read and check details. If what was chapter eight becomes chapter four, realize that you may have introduced new characters or facts in chapters five through seven that now will need to be established earlier. You'll also want to make certain that you have not revealed a part of the story too soon.

Moving passages in your writing may be necessary, but it can be a source of significant problems in your manuscript if you have not looked at all other affected parts of your book. To keep things rolling, it is generally easier to write the book sequentially. However, in some cases it may be more efficient to jump between chapters to connect certain concepts.

You are at a critical stage with your writing. If you have not yet finished, stay focused and keep going. The last 5-10% of the manuscript can be the most difficult, but you need to keep working since you are so close. Find someone to encourage you. Call on your support person or team and ask for help.

Day 7

Many of you will have a first draft written. If so, take a well-deserved break. Print the draft and put it away. Do not open the files on your computer or look at the hard copy for a few days. Go out and celebrate your accompliment.

If you have not finished, complete the first draft. Although this is designated a rest day, it is the last day of the four weeks; so you might want to make the final push and write through this session. If necessary add days to complete the draft, but try to keep your session short enough so you continue to the finish line. As I said, the final chapter or two can be challenging because you have to resolve all or most of the conflict and tie up loose ends. The finish line is in sight; so keep on task. When your draft is done, be sure to reward yourself.

Our Fiction Writer Dave

Day 1

Dave begins his week of writing by completing the estimated page count exercise. He determines that he will have to write 24 pages per day to finish the book in a week. He has timed himself and realizes if he is focused that he can write 12 pages in an hour. He decides he will extend his writing time to two hours a day and set the goal of reaching the end of the book in the allotted time.

He starts with the first chapter, "The Glimpse." Using his detailed outline, he begins writing about the main character, Franklin, who is having trouble getting to sleep. Just as he nods off, he is awakened by the strange lights that illuminate his room but do not seem to have a specific source. Dave next describes the sounds his character hears and how he gets up and goes to the window. He details the scene of his neighbor's apparent abduction as he watches him being sucked up into a vehicle that looks like a flying saucer. Unsure of what he has witnessed, he goes into the bathroom and splashes water on his face and then returns to the window. Everything outside appears completely normal; so Franklin decides it was some weird dream and returns to bed.

Dave then moves to the following chapter and writes about Franklin calling his best friend, Gregory, and his girlfriend, Barbara. He continues to try to get in touch throughout the day. He is a little worried when he is unable to contact them. Could they have decided to date and to leave Franklin behind? He calls other mutual friends and learns that they have not seen them either. Dave finishes the chapter as Franklin's search for the two of them continues.

Once Franklin realizes that they have not betrayed him, he gets all his friends together to try to find them. He introduces us to Amy and Bill who will become important characters. That completes the third chapter.

Dave can see the value of his plot outline. He returns to each chapter and includes background information about his characters and adds the Greensboro, North Carolina setting. He also writes descriptions of Franklin's house and that of his friends, Amy and Bill.

He looks at the time on his laptop and is pleased to see he has written for an hour-and-a-quarter. After saving his work, he determines he has written 5,500 words. He opens his WORD COUNT spreadsheet and enters the number. This equates to 22 pages. He feels satisfied although he knows he is a few pages short.

Day 2

Dave finishes classes and has dinner with Jean. He discusses how well he did on his first day of writing and explains that he will be less available this week. Jean asks to see what he's done so far, but, remembering that he needs to focus only on writing the draft, Dave refuses.

He does some homework and then about 7:30 opens the files on the laptop and continues writing. He creates the third and fourth chapters and part of the fifth and closes his writing file about 10 p.m. He has written 28 pages and is on track again. He lists today's tally in his WORD COUNT file.

The story is unfolding well and he adds four characters to his CHARACTERS file and three new entries to his SETTINGS file.

Day 3

Dave hides away in his favorite place in the library. A little weary from doing all the writing the day before and keeping up with his homework, he nonetheless remains determined to continue working through the rest of the week to complete his draft.

He returns to the "Meet Mr. Morse" chapter and finishes it as well as the remaining chapters in Part One of his book. He refers to his research document as he writes these, using the information he has gathered, to fill in the specifics about mindreading, telekinesis, flying saucers, space travel, space stasis and laser weapons.

Twenty-five pages later he performs his final save on the work, and counts the words. He enters these into his spreadsheet and updates his CHARACTERS and SETTINGS files. He has now written 74 pages, nearly half the book. He leaves the library at 11:00 p.m. and returns to the dorm to fall into bed. When he arrives, his roommate complains that he is never there. Dave responds that the writing will take only a few more days.

Day 4

Dave has decided to skip classes today to get a bigger chunk of his draft done. He writes the entire second part, "In Space." The project is now up to 112 pages. He saves the files and enters the day's total into the WORD COUNT file.

Day 5

Dave pushes ahead. He gets up early to work on the book, goes to classes, then returns to writing afterwards. He creates half of the remaining part, "Back On Earth." He logs his 20 pages and meets Jean for dinner.

His friend comments on how haggard he looks and he agrees. He tells Jean he now has written 132 pages and thinks he can complete the draft tomorrow or the next day. Knowing he will not have time to connect again until the task is behind him, they agree to meet and celebrate then.

Day 6

Dave can see the end is in sight. Again he decides to skip classes and focus on the book. He writes a few of the next chapters and falls asleep in front of his laptop in his room. When he awakens, he is too tired to continue; so he re-saves his chapter files and updates the others. He knows he needs some rest. He closes his door and sleeps until 9:00 p.m. After grabbing a bite to eat, he calls to update Jean and communicates that he will phone again tomorrow when he's done. Dave goes to bed, hoping he will have more energy in the morning.

Day 7

Unable to finish on the sixth day, Dave wakes up early on this Sunday morning and goes by the coffee house. He sits for 15 minutes and savors his cup of Kauai coffee and a sweet roll. He goes back to his room and sets up his laptop. His roommate is still sleeping. He opens his computer and file folders and gets ready to finish the book. He has only two chapters to go.

He feels fully awake and refreshed as he taps on the keys. The writing flows and before he knows it he has completed the next to last chapter. After getting up and stretching, he returns to the laptop and punches out the finale. He knows the writing isn't great for this chapter, but after his last words he saves his file.

Dave prints out his manuscript and puts it into a folder which he places into a drawer. With a wonderful smile on his face, he goes into the bathroom and looks in the mirror. He sees an unshaven, satisfied face looking back. He will clean up before he meets Jean.

He and Jean get together that evening. His writing buddy has cooked Dave his favorite meal, salmon fillet with white asparagus spears and double chocolate cake. They dine casually and then snuggle up on Jean's couch. Jean is proud of Dave for his accomplishment and asks again to read the manuscript.

"Soon," he replies, "soon. I need to do some spellchecking; then you can see it. You realize it's only the first draft though; so some of it is pretty rough."

"I understand," Jean replies, "but I still want to read it," she says and smiles slyly at him.

He hands the manuscript to her and she begins to read:

> *Franklin Trent turned over again under the amber colored sheet. He had kicked the thick, blue blanket to the floor to cool off. He could not keep his eyes closed and thought it was because he'd drunk too many cups of Kauai coffee. His redheaded girlfriend, Barbara, had given the beans to him as a gift because he loved strong coffee. Another sleepless night, he thought to himself. He searched for the reason his mind refused to rest but could not come up with one. Was there a new short story percolating in his brain?*
>
> *A few minutes later he felt his muscles relax and his eyelids shut. He began to drift off, but then it happened another time: His eyes opened and he was fully awake. Turning on his side, he stared at the shadows in the room. The half moon streamed light through the partially opened blinds, and he saw distorted outlines of his monitor and banker's lamp against the wall. He arose and closed the shades and these images became less distinguishable. He drifted off again.*
>
> *His newly acquired state of sleep was interrupted as he turned on his side with a foreboding feeling. He cursed his imagination and told it to go back to sleep.*

No more ideas for stories. He relaxed into an alpha state again and felt he could doze off.

He sensed a bright light on his eyelids and tried to coax himself back to sleep. The light would not go away so he slowly opened his eyes. The room was dark, nothing accounting for the sensation he had just experienced. He cursed the coffee once more and closed his lids.

For a second time the brightness disturbed him and now when he opened his eyes, the room was bathed in an unnatural orange light. The duration was longer than a blink and lasted over a minute, then extinguished itself. A shiver shook him as Franklin bolted upright. He tried to adjust his eyes to the shadows in the once-more dark bedroom.

He lay there for minutes in the semi-darkness until he heard a set of unfamiliar sounds. First he perceived what sounded like an industrial engine powering up, then the release of steam. Next came the cracking of metal scraping as if some massive chasm was opening followed by a hydraulic release. And the light turned to lime green.

He leaped over to the window and almost tripped on a pile of school books. He squeezed open the blinds and his pupils contracted to adjust to the glare. He saw a beam of putrid green light emanating from something in the sky darting down into the house next door. The light beam and the vessel above phased in and out. He pinched himself to be sure he was awake as he continued to stare. Was this some new fiction he was fabricating from a dream?

After the Draft

Congratulations! Now that you have finished writing your draft, put it away for one to seven days and then read it from a fresh perspective—as a reader, not the writer. Next, you will want to complete three tasks before sending your manuscript to a publisher or publishing it yourself:

- Self-edit and send it to someone else to edit.
- Format as an e-book or for traditional printing or submit to a publisher with cover letter.
- Plan and execute publicity.

I easily could and may write books about all of these topics, but in this chapter I will briefly describe each of them.

EDIT

Finishing that first draft requires a bit of a sprint. Once you have completed the draft, set it aside for at least several days. When you pull the manuscript out of the drawer, approach it as if someone else wrote it. You might want to read it four times before getting someone else to look at it.

Editing your own material can be difficult and is rarely as much fun as writing the book. To save money you need to review your manuscript a number of times before submitting it to a professional editor. Editors with whom I have worked ask for a sample to evaluate the job and ascertain how much time and work will be needed; from that they create a price estimate.

When you are ready to work on your manuscript, read it for:

- Continuity
- Logic
- Impact
- Grammar, spelling and punctuation

First, read for continuity. When a team makes a movie, the script supervisor plays a vital role. During filming, that person watches what is happening to be sure that characters are wearing the same clothes during a scene, that the props are placed in identical places, that hair styles are as they were in previous shots. You need to play a similar role in the editing of your book. When you read for continuity, be certain your ideas and presentation are consistent. Be sure that all the concepts follow naturally and that you have continuity in all elements including tense, person and voice.

Read for logic. Does the book make sense? Does the plotline flow correctly? Do your readers want to begin the next chapter at the end of the previous one? Is the action scripted in the correct order? Have you arranged the chapters in the easiest sequence to understand?

Are storyline, references to settings and character and descriptions written in such a way that the reader will understand what is happening in later chapters? Check to determine if any of these are missing because this can happen if you moved chapters.

Read for impact. When you edit the third time, be sure you are presenting your story with the greatest effect. Check each sentence to consider whether you made the best word choices and expressed these in the most ideal order. Look to see that every sentence carries the reader to the next. Each chapter ending should make the reader want to move to the following one with curiosity and anticipation.

Read for grammar and spelling. Finally, edit for grammar, punctuation and spelling errors. Do not rely solely on your word processor's spelling and grammar checking. Spell checkers cannot catch the words that are different from the ones you intended to use. Properly spelled words are often wrong by only one letter (hot/hit, few/fee, in/on, of/off, etc.) but hard for the author to see. Look for errors on your own. Confirm that you have only one space between sentences.

Many writers don't remember all the punctuation rules especially those about commas. If you need a refresher, find an online reference or a book that describes the use and rules of punctuation. Check your spelling carefully. Make sure you have written complete sentences (unless you are sure that a sentence fragment conveys all of your meaning). Readers may be critical of your writing if you use incomplete sentences even if you like writing this way.

When you do the final self-edit, be aware that the human mind fills in the blanks or missing information. Nowhere is this more dangerous for us writers than when we re-read our own work. Our brains tend to see what we *think* we wrote. Check all these editing steps, especially the last one, with that in mind.

FORMAT/SUBMISSION FOR SELF-PUBLISHED OR SMALL PRESS WORKS

The format for your book is dictated by the platform and the publisher or printer. There are significant differences between formatting for an e-book versus traditional paperback and hardback book printing.

The Internal Pages E-book

If you are publishing an e-book, you will need to learn which file formats are accepted by Amazon, Barnes & Noble or any other online publisher. Amazon will accept *Microsoft Word* unfiltered *.html* files or a *.mobi* file. If your book has complex internal formatting, you may need to get help from an outside source who can program those difficult sections.

The Internal Pages Print

For print book publishing, you will have to determine the size of your book and number of pages as well as other specifications including fonts, margins, gutters and more. Will you have perfect binding (with a spine with printing on it) or another type? Will the book be a paperback or hardback?

Formatting the Inside of Your Book

You can learn to format your text and graphics for the inside of your book yourself or hire someone to do this for you. E-books are easy enough to build unless there is complex formatting. In that case, you might need to enlist the help of a programmer. Print books, on the other hand, take more expertise, and you may want to get help from someone who can build your book in a professional program like *Adobe InDesign*™.

I formatted my first e-books and am happy that I did. However, there was a learning curve with the software although not as steep as the one with a professional product like *InDesign*. Amazon has created software to help you publish your e-book; however, you must be cautious if you have pictures. You may have to find a programmer to ensure that those appear correctly.

Cover Creation

They say you can't judge a book by the cover, but in today's competitive world you need a cover that will attract the attention of potential readers. My first non-fiction book had a self-designed cover. I'm a writer, not a designer, and my original home-made cover reflected that. I needed to get the book out quickly and did not allow time or budget to have one designed for me. I have since had a professional graphic artist create a cover for this entire series. My books now look as professional on the outside as they are on the inside.

The Cover

You will need graphics for your book cover.

For an e-book, this is usually a high-resolution *.jpg*. Different print publishers and printers will ask for a *.pdf* file or a *.jpg* with specific margins, gutters and pre-sets for a *.pdf*. You will be required to deliver a separate file for the cover.

Submitting Your Book for Traditional Publishing

When your manuscript is accepted by a traditional publisher, they will take care of the formatting for print and e-book editions. Initially, you must present your writing in their suggested format to even have the book considered. Preparing work for a traditional publisher is beyond the scope of this book, but you begin by finding out what the publisher wants and writing a compelling cover letter. One source for learning this information is *Writer's Market,* which comes out with a new edition annually.

PUBLICITY

Begin letting people know about your book while you are still writing it. Once your novel is published, doing publicity is critical. You must advertise your book if you want it to earn money and/or enhance your reputation. For authors who are introverts—and many work in solitude and tend to be at least inwardly motivated—this can be a challenging step. *No one can sell a book like the author.* Even with a traditional publisher, unless you are a well-known writer, you will not get much help publicizing your book. If you opt in to paid-for publicity, which some independent publishers offer, you will still be the best salesperson for your novel.

After I self-published a poetry book, I went to all the local booksellers and asked them to carry it. Only a few—mostly independent stores—agreed to stock it for me. They took the book on consignment, and it was my responsibility to check back weekly or monthly to collect any profits from sales. Today you can sell online through Amazon, which wasn't a possibility at that time. Nevertheless, just uploading your e-book or putting it up for sale is not enough. You will need to be *the best salesperson* for your own work. Consider reading at bookstores and libraries.

You can use social media, but most authors I know begin by selling their own books person to person. If it catches on, Amazon can help as well as other organizations. Try local newspapers and magazines. You may want to take out an ad in one of those publications.

Remember during week one that we visualized an interview? Now is the time to set up a session with local radio and television stations. You also may want to arrange an interview with a host who has an internet platform such as Blogspot or iHeartRadio.

Get creative. Consider where your readers are and find a means to connect with them. What Meetup.com groups in your area would be interested in having you speak? Are there other organizations you could approach who would be attracted to your topic? Remember to build your marketing around your avatar.

Allow your readers to interact with you. Develop a relationship with your audience so you can build a raving fan base.

Enjoy your author status and have fun with your book. You have put forth great effort, and I wish you all the rewards you can think of for yourself.

Resources

Footnotes:

[1] Wallace Wattles (1910) *The Science of Getting Rich* Holyoke, Mass: Elizabeth Towne Company.

[2] Stephen Covey (2004) *The 7 Habits of Highly Effective People* New York: Simon & Shuster.

[3] Orson Scott Card (1988) *Characters and Viewpoint* Cincinnati: Writer's Digest Books.

[4] Robert McKee *Story* (1997) ReganBooks; 1 edition (November 25, 1997).

Here are a few resources I recommend:

Characters and Viewpoint by Orson Scott Card

Story: Substance, Structure, Style and the Principles of Screenwriting by Robert McKee

Elements of Style by William Strunk

Rules for Writers by Diana Hacker

A Manual of Style on University of Chicago Press

Writer's Market

These are the files mentioned in this book:

- FIRST VISUALIZATION file
- WRITING ENVIRONMENT file
- AVATAR file
- BOOK LAUNCH file
- INTERVIEW file
- PURPOSE file
- MAJOR CHARACTER file
- MINOR CHARACTER file
- PERSPECTIVE 1 file
- PERSPECTIVE 2 file
- PERSPECTIVE 3 file
- PLOT file
- SETTINGS file
- AUDIENCE RESEARCH file
- CONTENT RESEARCH file
- WORD COUNT file

BONUS: Email the author for templates for these files at Drew@RealizationPress.com.

ACCOUNTABILITY

Do you need help to stay on course? I provide clients with a Writing Accountability Program: For more information go to drewbecker.com/accountability.

Other books by the Author:

Poetry

I Fell for 13 Dreamers

Writers Block Series

Book 1
Interviewing Quick Guide: The Art and Craft
Book 2
Write a Non-Fiction Book in 4 Weeks

Coming Soon

Book 4
Personal Branding for Writers and Speakers (working title)

www.ingramcontent.com/pod-product-compliance
Lightning Source LLC
Chambersburg PA
CBHW071719020426
42333CB00017B/2333